Come to Hong Kong!

By Cameron Macintosh

Come to Hong Kong!

You can do a lot of fun things.

You can get dishes like duck wings and dim sum.

You can get hot pot, which is a thin but rich broth.

It is fun to shop
in Hong Kong.

Lots of shops hang things up
to get you to come
into them.

This spot has lots of little shops.

They sell a lot of things.

You can walk up this track.

Do not rush!

It is a long track.

When you get to the top, you can check out all of Hong Kong!

You can see a man sing some songs.

Bang! Zing! Ping!

Hong Kong is so much fun!

CHECKING FOR MEANING

1. What can you eat in Hong Kong? *(Literal)*
2. Why do lots of shops hang things out the front? *(Literal)*
3. Why should you not rush up the long track? *(Inferential)*

EXTENDING VOCABULARY

hot pot	The words *hot* and *pot* rhyme. What other words do you know that rhyme with these words?
hang	What are the sounds in the word *hang*? What other words do you know that rhyme with *hang*?
sing	What other words do you know that are related to the word *sing*?

MOVING BEYOND THE TEXT

1. What is your favourite place to visit near where you live?
2. Which country or city would you most like to visit? Why?
3. What foods do you know that come from other countries? Have you tried any of these foods?
4. Would you like to visit Hong Kong? Why?

SPEED SOUNDS

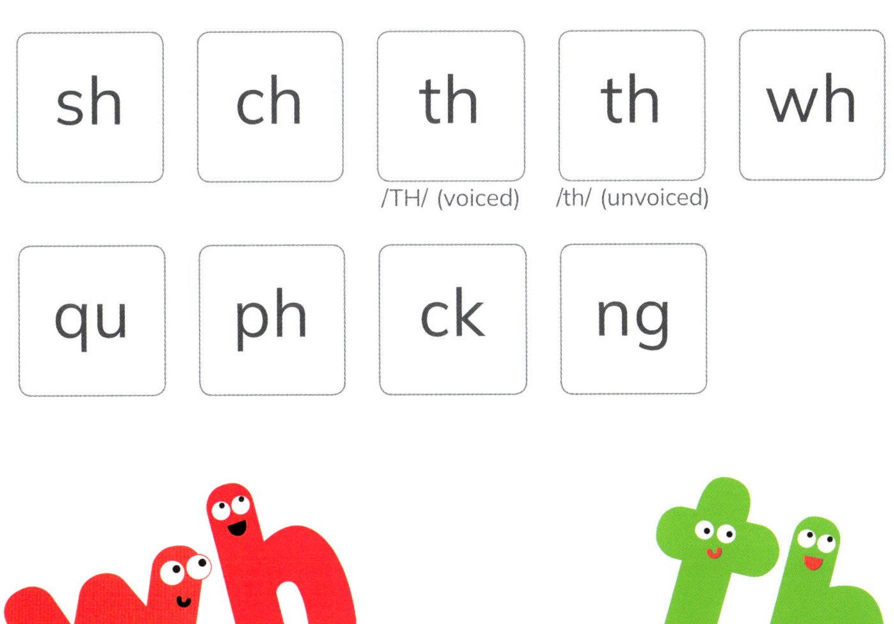

PRACTICE WORDS

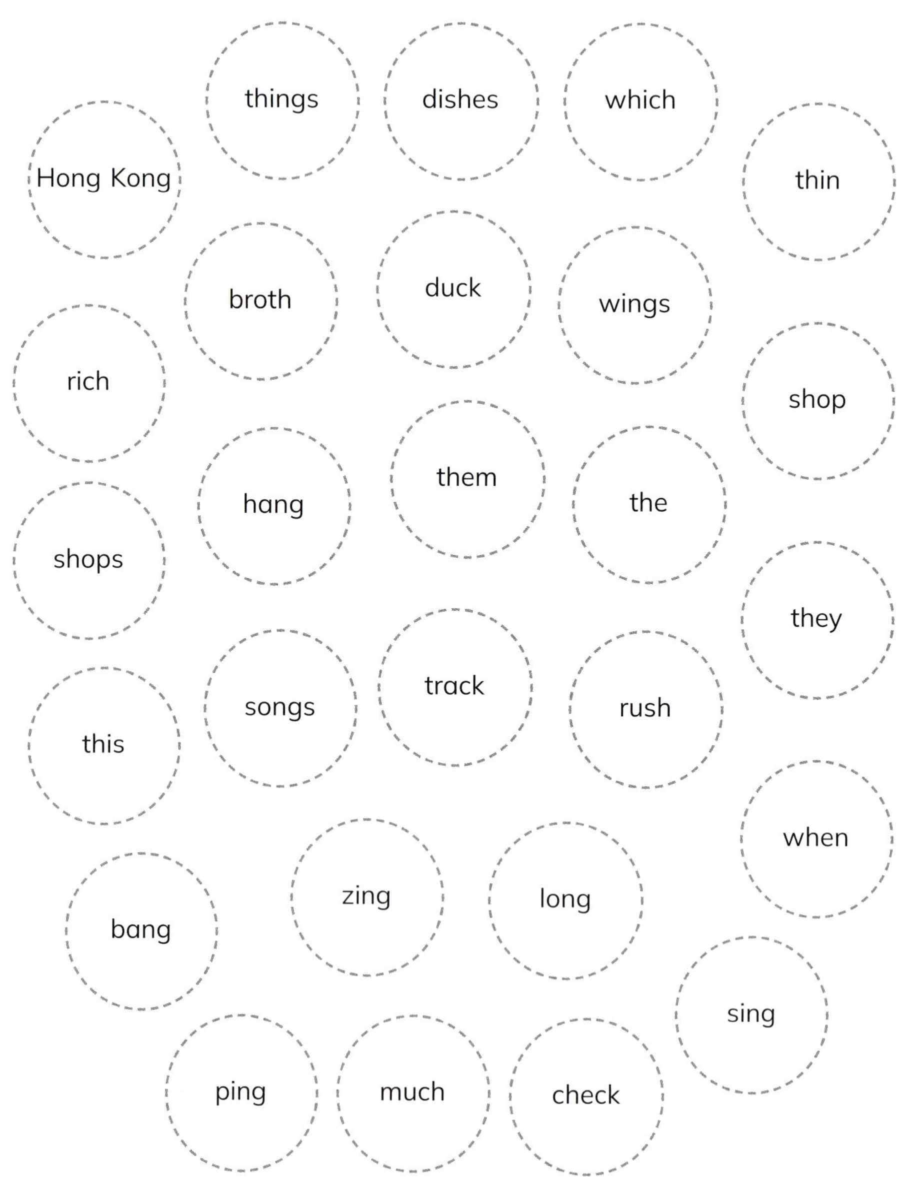